IMAGES
of England

AROUND
WENDOVER
AND HALTON

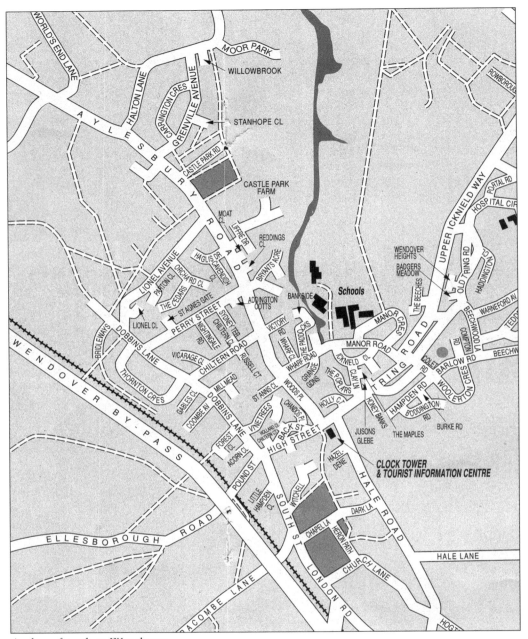

A plan of modern Wendover.

IMAGES
of England

AROUND
WENDOVER
AND HALTON

Compiled by
Paul Dabrowski
Captions by
John How

TEMPUS

Tempus Publishing Limited
The Mill, Brimscombe Port,
Stroud, Gloucestershire, GL5 2QG

ISBN 0 7524 1694 4

Typesetting and origination by
Tempus Publishing Limited
Printed in Great Britain by
Midway Clark Printing, Wiltshire

A multi-view postcard of Wendover from between the wars, showing, clockwise from the top left: the Manor Waste, St Mary's church, Anne Boleyn's Cottages and the Corner House and Aylesbury Road. In the centre is the monument on Coombe Hill.

Contents

Aylesbury Road from the top of the Clock Tower, in the early 1980s.

Introduction

Wendover is a place of beauty, nestling in the Chiltern Hills. It is only thirty-six miles from London, on the edge of what was once called 'Metroland', but this proximity to the capital is not to be noticed as one strolls through the village and into the hills beyond. This is Buckinghamshire countryside at its best. Gaze down Wendover High Street as it descends towards the Clock Tower, with Boddington Hill, the woods and Halton beyond – where could you find a more magnificent scene?

The appeal of Wendover runs deeper than the beauty of its setting. The village has a history dating back to pre-Roman times. The Icknield Way is an ancient Iron Age trackway which runs from East Anglia through Wendover *en route* to the Thames crossing at Goring. Beyond this it becomes the Ridgeway, a major ancient route to south-west England. There are remains of earthworks nearby, notably Grims Dyke, which date from before the Roman invasion in AD 43. The name of Wendover recalls its Celtic connections. It is one of the few placenames in southern England to have undeniably Celtic roots; it comes from the same origin as the modern Welsh *gwyn dwr*, meaning 'white water'. The Danes were here too, in the ninth and tenth centuries, as Wendover was not far from the boundary of the Danelaw.

Moving on through the centuries, Wendover became a 'rotten and pocket borough' which elected two Members of Parliament despite its small population. Among these were John Hampden the Patriot, MP in 1623, and John Wilkes. John Hampden is commemorated to this day in a street name in the village. The parliamentary connection with the area is still maintained: just outside Wendover towards Ellesborough is Chequers, the country home of the Prime Ministers of the United Kingdom.

The Rothschild family has a strong connection with the Chilterns. Famous for their connections with Tring, they also built a mansion at Halton, which brought much employment and prosperity to the area. The mansion was taken over by the military during the First World War for use as a training camp: the officers stayed in the mansion itself while the other ranks were accommodated in tents in the extensive grounds. After the war, the estate passed into the hands of the newly-formed RAF. A large camp evolved, complete with barracks, workshops and hangars; it was used primarily for training apprentices on aircraft maintenance. Halton and Wendover therefore became known to RAF servicemen from far and wide.

The most historic event of modern times has been the construction of the Wendover bypass. Villagers first started to fight for it in the 1960s, but it was eventually opened only in 1998. It is a tribute to the determination of Wendover's County Councillor, Frank Goodson, who died in 1999. The bypass has not stopped people coming to Wendover, Gateway to the Chilterns; instead it has made it easier and safer.

This is not the only Wendover in the world. In the United States there is another Wendover, part in Utah, part in Nevada. Although the salt flats of the American town are a far cry from the hills of the Buckinghamshire village, there is a similarity: Wendover, USA has a US Air Force base next door. Closer to home Wendover, Bucks is twinned with Liffre in France and there is a twinning stone outside the local library to commemorate this. This union has resulted in a fruitful companionship between the two villages and their inhabitants.

The first six chapters take the form of a tour through Wendover itself, ending with a miscellany of pictures from around the town. The people of Wendover past and present are commemorated in Chapter Seven and the final two chapters move further afield, through the surrounding Chiltern Hills and on to Halton.

One
High Street and Back Street

Looking down the High Street towards the Clock Tower, with Boddington Hill beyond. The road surface is still unmetalled, the drains are open and the lamps are gas; hence the date is probably around 1900.

Early in the twentieth century a stage coach used to run to London, stopping to pick up Wendover passengers outside the Red Lion Hotel, seen here. It was just a nostalgic reminder of times gone by, as Wendover had had a direct rail service to London for many years.

The High Street, Clock Tower and Boddington woods behind, c. 1902. This is the beautiful view described in the Introduction. The traditional horse and cart now has to share the road with a primitive motor car, probably one of the first to be seen in Wendover.

Safely aboard the stage to London, the traveller's journey is unlikely to be obstructed by traffic. The young lad in the road could easily play with a spinning top or hoop without disturbance. The shop on the right was then Smith's butchers; the building still stands but now houses a dress shop. There is a hairdresser's next door.

A group of Edwardian girls prepare to cross the High Street by the Swan public house. Just beyond is the Two Brewers, now a restaurant. There was a brewery on the opposite side of the road.

Two parties stop for refreshment at the King's Head, towards the end of the nineteenth century. Holland's is a well-known name in Wendover. The sign below indicates that cycling trips were a popular form of recreation. The King's Head is sadly no longer in existence.

This is the Manor Waste as it used to be, where Wendover's war memorial now stands. In the days when farmers herded sheep on foot rather than by train or lorry, they used to pause in this useful open space in Wendover, on their way to Aylesbury market or to fresh fields. The trees and sheep create a rural image which is scarcely imaginable today.

The High Street and Manor Waste in the late 1920s. Although the sheep are gone, there is still a predominantly rural aspect to this view.

The Manor Waste today. Farmers stopped using the area to rest their beasts as they could be more easily transported by lorry, so the Waste became neglected and its surface dangerous. Concerned about this, Wendover Parish Council put the problem to the Lord of the Manor, Mr Lionel Abel-Smith, and he donated several thousands of pounds to renovate it. It was suggested at the time that the square be called the 'Wendover Environmental Area' – 'environment' being a buzz-word at the time – but fortunately tradition and history prevailed and the Manor Waste it remains.

Wendover war memorial, erected after the First World War. The lower picture shows the extent of the renovation carried out in recent years, but the general surroundings have changed little.

A last look at the Red Lion. This remains a popular hostelry to this day. The frontage has changed little since this photograph was taken. Rumour has it that Oliver Cromwell stayed here once.

A tranquil, rural scene with a good view of the old chimneys of the cottages opposite. Down a lane to the right was Floyd's undertakers and the village smithy, run by Freddie Birch.

The Two Brewers, the Swan and at the far end the Clock Tower on a quiet day around the turn of the century.

A very early view of the High Street from the old Literary Institute. When horses and carts were the norm, many men were employed 'dunging'. They would collect the droppings from the horses and sell them on as manure for farmers' fields.

The same corner today, with a constant flow of traffic. The buildings have changed surprisingly little in the hundred years or more that separate these views; a couple of shop frontages have been altered and the growth of ivy on the right has gone, but little else is different.

Wendover High Street in the 1950s. There is a good mixture of styles and ages of vehicle to be seen; some of them probably date from before the Second World War, at a time when people changed their cars far less frequently than today.

A similar view from the 1960s. By the Manor Waste (on the left, in use as a car park) is the National Provincial Bank, one of the forerunners of the NatWest; the building is no longer a bank.

A busy shopping day in the High Street in the 1970s. The Clock Tower, here framed by the hills and trees, is now the office of Wendover Parish Council and also houses the tourist information centre for the 'Gateway to the Chilterns'.

The Clock Tower has seen a variety of uses over the years. Before it became the Council Offices and tourist information centre, it was the storage place for the corporation dustcart. At that time, to call the fire brigade, one had to get the key, open up the tower and ring the fire bell inside. Shortly after the Second World War, pigeons took to roosting in the tower. Their droppings froze on the workings of the clock, which went 'off-strike', so the council had to install netting in the belfry to keep the birds out. No doubt they have moved on to 'decorate' some other premises!

A Wendover scene that is no more: the fair that was held twice yearly, in May and October, on the Manor Waste. After the war, a dispute arose between the Guild of Showmen and the Parish Council over who had the rights to run the fair. The Council obtained from the Muniments Room of the British Museum a copy of the charter. When translated from the Latin it 'granted the right of the Citizens and Burgesses of Wendover that a fair be holden on two feast days...'. The showmen were there only by traditional usage, so they came every May and October to preserve this right. In days gone by, the fun fairs would have combined with the cattle fairs – such a mixture must have created chaos in the High Street!

Back Street towards the end of the nineteenth century. On the right is the old Village Pump, the only source of water for drinking, cooking and washing for most people before the advent of mains plumbing.

THE OLD VILLAGE PUMP, BACK STREET, WENDOVER

A slightly later view of Back Street. The Wendover skyline has begun to sprout telegraph poles, but the pump is still in daily use. The cottage on the left has a pear tree standing by it, and on the right beyond the pump are the back entrances to the Two Brewers pub (now a restaurant) and the Swan.

Back Street today, without the pump. At the bottom of the street, where it joins the Aylesbury Road, is a huge stone, nestling by the Corner House. Some say it is a volcanic stone; whatever its origin, it has been there for eighty years and more.

Two
Pound Street and the Railway

Pound Street in the early years of the twentieth century. The Shoulder of Mutton pub on the left was also known as the Railway Hotel.

A slightly later view of Pound Street, probably during the 1930s. The pub has dropped its Shoulder of Mutton title in favour of the railway connection. The railway is immediately behind the camera, with the Ellesborough Road and Coombe Hill beyond.

Pound Street today, with the pub restored to its original name. The railway line is now accompanied by the Wendover bypass, which passes beneath a new bridge on the Ellesborough Road, behind the camera.

A view from the High Street into Pound Street, 1930s. The signposted turning on the left is the London Road; this junction is controlled by a roundabout today.

The old thatched cottages on Pound Street, opposite the Shoulder of Mutton. These picturesque dwellings are still some of the first buildings the traveller sees on entering Wendover from the west.

Pound Street in snow, looking towards the High Street. The old railway bridge is on the right.

Wendover station from the Ellesborough Road bridge.

This temporary bridge over the railway was erected during the construction of the new bridge (which can be seen to the right). These developments accompanied the building of the bypass during 1998. Wendover's County Councillor, Frank Goodson, was instrumental in getting the bypass built. Sadly he died in early 1999 but his memory lives on: the new bridge is called Goodson's Bridge. Paul Dabrowski is standing on the temporary bridge.

A leisurely stroll with the dog and a brief outing on horseback over the old railway bridge before the bypass was built.

The same view today, with the bypass running parallel to the railway beneath the Ellesborough Road.

Three
Tring Road

Coldharbour. Wendover.

Coldharbour cottages on the Tring Road. Bank Farm is on the right.

The Anne Boleyn Cottages, so called because they were given by Henry VIII to his second wife in the brief period that they were married (she was later executed). This photograph dates from the era of unsurfaced roads and horse-drawn traffic; it is probably pre-1920.

A modern view of the Anne Boleyn Cottages. The road is now lined with parked cars and the cottages have been given a smart coat of whitewash.

The other end of the row of half-timbered cottages, showing part of the historic Pack Horse inn.

A happy group of Edwardian ladies and children gather in the sun on the Tring Road. This appears to be a posed photograph, as most of those present are looking at the camera. At this period the arrival of a photographer in the village would have created widespread interest.

Tring Road cottages in the snow in more recent times.

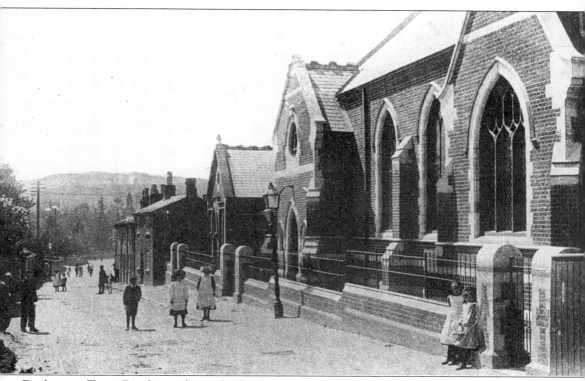

Further up Tring Road, just beyond Clay Lane, once stood the Wendover Congregational church. This was where a member of Ramsay Macdonald's family was married, when Ramsay himself was Prime Minister. Ramsay Macdonald achieved fame as the first Labour Prime Minister in 1924. The church has since been demolished and houses now stand in its place.

The corner shop where the Tring Road (right) meets the Aylesbury Road (left), *c.* 1890. Among the advertisements for Venus and Sunlight Soaps and Colman's Starch there is a rather unusual notice erected by Wendover Parish Council, just below the sign for Tring. It reads: 'CAUTION. Persons removing Gravel, Sand or other Materials from the Highways will be Prosecuted.'

A patriotic display of flags on the Tring Road and a good turn-out of villagers greet the motorcade for the wedding of Miss Macdonald, the daughter of Prime Minister Ramsay Macdonald. The ceremony took place at the Congregational church further up the road.

Further up the Tring Road used to be the White House Tea Rooms, where many a lorry driver would stop for a bite to eat and a cup of tea. Now the lorries no longer stop, passing Wendover by on the bypass, and the café has been replaced by flats.

At the top of the hill on Tring Road was the Camp Studio, which dealt with many of the photographic requirements of RAF Halton and Wendover as well. The old Four Seasons pub is opposite.

The old Camp Studio building is no more. Instead there are homes and gardens, part of the Honeydene Estate, and a wider road.

Four
Aylesbury Road

The Clock Tower seen from the Aylesbury Road. Note the horse trough by the right-hand side of the tower: this has since been removed.

A picturesque view down Aylesbury Road to the George Inn and the Clock Tower. Despite the lack of traffic there is still a 10mph speed limit in force. There are soldiers in uniform walking around in the distance: this dates the picture to the years around the First World War, when Halton was used as a training camp.

The same view around fifty years later. The old Wendover fire station used to be on the right next to the black and white half-timbered house and just on that corner was Freddie Thorne's barber shop. He and his son, Arnold, also an enthusiastic member of the fire brigade, would give a 'short back and sides' for fourpence and a shave for twopence.

Closer to the Clock Tower, before either motor cars or speed limits. On the left is the George Inn and to the left of this were the Parish Rooms. The Clock Tower now houses the Parish Council's offices.

The corner of Aylesbury Road and Tring Road, last seen on p. 36. The number of uniformed soldiers waiting to buy refreshments and pass the time of day in Mrs Morgan's sweet shop suggests that this photograph dates from the First World War.

AYLESBURY ST., & CLOCK TOWER, WENDOVER.

The baker on his rounds with his assistant and horse and cart, probably before the First World War. The village doctor lived and practised nearby in later years.

Two contrasting views of the Aylesbury Road corner with Tring Road. The old shop has given way to a modern off-licence and modern traffic has necessitated the creation of a roundabout. The curious notice on the side of the corner shop has disappeared and the Tring Road frontage has been extensively modified. Now, in 1999, the off-licence seems set to become a restaurant.

The 'Tea and Dining Rooms' on the Aylesbury Road, known as the Corner House Hotel.

For years the George Inn, opposite the Corner House Hotel, had only a six-day licence. It was said to be owned by the Church, which frowned upon drinking on Sundays. However, it was evidently open on this day in the 1960s when a cyclist popped in for a quick pint!

Further down and just off Aylesbury Road is Wendover's old windmill. It stopped working in 1926 and was turned into a private residence; it was around this time that it lost its sails. It also had a supplementary steam engine to drive the corn-grinding machinery.

The mill when it was still working, around the turn of the century. The mill-workers are Toby Wood (left), Ernest Buggey (right) and Frank Purssell, the owner (on the balcony).

The mill engine being broken up after the mill was closed, *c*. 1928.

The mill, now sail-less, seen from the Tring Road in 1980.

Five

The Heron Path
and the Church

The Heron Path on a frosty morning in the 1990s. Note the new footbridge on the right.

THE MILL STREAM, WENDOVER.

The Mill Stream and Heron Path at the same place as the picture on p. 47 but nearly 100 years earlier. There is no bridge over the stream and the lighting is provided by the prominent gas lamp. The Heron Path has always been a popular route for villagers to take to St Mary's parish church. In recent years it has become more widely popular, being walked by thousands of visitors each year, as the path forms a part of the famous Ridgeway long-distance footpath which runs from Ivinghoe Beacon in Buckinghamshire to near Avebury in Wiltshire.

The Herring Path, Wendover
63850

A pair of Victorian ladies take a stroll alongside the Mill Stream to give the baby some air. The pram is typical of the period, with high, narrow wheels. There is something 'fishy' about the original caption to this postcard: the way is called the Heron Path, not the 'Herring Path'!

The houses to the east of the Heron Path once housed Wendover Church of England Senior and Junior Schools. Here a group of schoolgirls take a break from lessons in the fields nearby probably during the Edwardian period. The old school buildings are visible in the background to the left; the right-hand building, further away, is the old water mill, now also converted into a private dwelling.

This view of the Heron Path nearer to the church shows a Mill Stream which is far wider than it is today. The small building is no longer in existence.

The Sluice Cottage stands next to the Heron Path and Mill Stream, nestling in pleasant rural surroundings. In the background is some pleasant rolling Chiltern scenery.

A closer look at Sluice Cottage, with a view of the waterfall.

Along the Mill Stream stands Bucksbridge House. This is a majestic house with a fine garden.

Two views, old and not so old, of Bucksbridge Farm alongside the Mill Stream. Little seems to have changed between the two views. Note the pump on the chimney-breast side of the house: this would have provided the only source of fresh water in the days before mains plumbing. There have since been considerable changes to what was once a farm cottage.

The London Road, seen here around 1920. Although long-distance traffic now uses the bypass, it is still one of the busiest roads in Wendover.

St Mary's parish church tower seen from across Hampden Pond, near the Heron Path.

The church from the other side, showing the well-tended churchyard. Recently there have been problems with the church bells.

Another look at St Mary's church, this time from the lich-gate side. A local legend has it that the church was moved by fairies or witches to its present site from Witchell, which is a corruption of 'witch well'. The church has another claim to fame: in the early nineteenth century the first National Savings Bank was founded by the Revd Joseph Smith and operated from the church's vestry.

The interior of St Mary's church during a service.

Six

Hopping About the Village

During the First World War the YMCA had a hut in the playground of the Church of England school, next to the Heron Path. After the war it was moved down the Aylesbury Road to Bryants Acre, where it became the focus of entertainment in Wendover. There was plenty of dancing in those days, and to make the dance floor smoother, bath salts were strewn over the floorboards! The room was heated by two old tortoise stoves, so when the place warmed up, it was permeated by a bathroom scent. It became well-known to airmen from RAF Halton and others as the 'Old Sweat Box' and many ex-servicemen from far and wide have fond memories of it.

The old Nag's Head inn on the Tring Road. This is no longer a public house, although the building remains.

Not far from another hostelry at the other end of town: this is the view down Pound Street from the Ellesborough Road. The Railway Hotel (or Shoulder of Mutton) is not far away.

D.L. Norris's Grocery and Provision Stores at Scrubwood in Victorian times. In addition to selling groceries and provisions, copious advertisements next to the door show that teas and refreshments could be obtained at 6d a time. Scrubwood is now known as Dunsmore.

Mrs Fox, the appropriately named landlady of The Fox at Scrubwood, used to provide excellent cream teas to Edwardian day-trippers. Note that the name of the area used to be Scrubb's Wood – here is evidence that English placenames are still evolving and changing.

The Thirty Cottages, otherwise known as York Buildings, on the Tring Road. This view dates from around the time of the First World War.

Wellwick Farm, off the Ellesborough Road. This historic building dates from the seventeenth century. The notorious Judge Jeffreys is said to have hidden here after conducting the Bloody Assizes at Dorchester, at which he sentenced to death many of those involved in the revolt by the Duke of Monmouth against James II.

The old sluice on Wharf Road, at the start of the canal. No doubt the village children spent many an enjoyable day swimming and playing in this attractive rural landscape.

Today, children are more likely to take to the water in the up-to-date open-air swimming pool at John Colet School. Since this picture was taken, the pool has been given a retractable roof.

At the Aylesbury end of Wendover is Halton Reservoir. In days gone by this would have been a popular bathing area for local youngsters, but today it is the haunt of anglers and those who go sailing.

Not far from Halton Reservoir is the End of the World public house, previously known as The Swan, situated in an area known as World's End. This name is a corruption of 'wold's end', or the end of the cattle-grazing land of Wendover.

A last look at Hampden Pond, with the church tower in the distance. On this occasion the water level became so low that the pond was completely drained.

South Street early in the twentieth century. This dates from an era when personal transport took the form of a bicycle or 'Shanks's pony', while larger loads were hauled by horse and cart, such as the one coming into view in the distance. James Cameron, the famous BBC correspondent, lived in the tall house on the left when he was a schoolboy.

Wendover Church of England School. The school was built in 1879. The building survives to this day, although no longer as a school; both it and the infants' school next door have since been divided into private houses.

The playground of the old Church of England School in the 1960s.

The former Baptist chapel on South Street (London Road). It has now been divided into flats.

All the fun of the fair! A travelling fair visits Wendover High Street in 1967. However, it does not match the old cattle fairs that used to be held in Wendover.

Two views from villages not far from Wendover, showing the rural nature of the area's surroundings. *Above:* Thatched cottages at Butlers Cross, Ellesborough. *Below:* The Crown Inn at Little Kimble. The sacks could contain flour destined for the village bakery.

Seven

People

A statue of John Hampden, Wendover's MP in 1623.

Fun is being had by all at this cheese and wine evening in Wendover Memorial Hall in February 1970.

The Wendover Brownies line up smartly for a group photograph with their leaders.

Boys from the John Colet School display the produce they have grown, 1967. The boys third and fourth from the left are Paul Ellis and Terry Grimsdale.

The Hunt (possibly the Old Berkeley) rides through Wendover, probably during the 1930s.

Before the Second World War, the Church of England School had gardens just up the Heron Path, where the children were taught the basics of horticulture. Here a group of smartly dressed Edwardian schoolgirls pose with a variety of garden implements.

Edwardian children learn all about horticulture in the gardens of Wendover Church of England School.

The school gardens some years later. The children have paused to receive further instructions from the headmaster, Arthur Mollineux, in the straw boater.

The Dabrowski family outside their home at Calloway on Boddington Hill in 1954. The house, which at one time was called Peacock Farm, has since been demolished. From left to right, back row: Mrs Mavis Dabrowski, Mrs Violet Cable, Rodney Cable. Front row: Susan, Paul, Danny and David Dabrowski.

Wendover Football Club in 1897, a year after it became affiliated to the Berks and Bucks Football Association.

Standard I at Wendover Church of England School in 1922. Among those pictured are Ron Heels, Herbert Ridgeway, Norman Hibberd, Henry Moore, Doris Saunders, Len Warner, Nora Hudson and Arthur 'Dicky' Bird. The lad holding the card in the front row is John How.

The 1st Wendover Scout Troop in 1928. They were a very successful troop, winning titles in boxing, football and cross-country at the Bucks County Championship. They went on an annual camping trip for a fortnight to Jersey; at first this cost £1 per Scout but later went up to £1 10s. From left to right, back row: Fred Harding, Sid Gurney (?), Harry Harding, Robert 'Sonny' Goodwin, 'Tunkie' Tew, Joe Gorley. Third row: Fred Parsons, Horace Pratt, Charlie Freeman, Jack Floyd, George Pratt, Jim Sherriff, Alf Sawtell, Fred Oakley, Billy Dembon, George Gorley. Second row: Ron Heels, Norman Hibberd, John How, Tom Smith, Cyril Woodward, Harry Floyd, Harold Caudrey, Len Warner, Bill Turney, Bob Westmore, Harry Moore, Ron Dupoix, Eddie Riley. Front row: John King, Ron Philbey, ? Pendry, K. Cameron, -?-, John Day, Stan Watson, Vic Birch, Peter Eldridge, Alan Pendry, ? Daniels, Jim Atkins.

Eight

Chilterns and Chequers

Two soldiers enjoy a stroll in Wendover Woods.

Wendover lies in the so-called Wendover Gap in the Chilterns. To the west is Coombe Hill, seen here in deep snow and sparkling conditions.

Boddington Hill flanks Wendover on the east. The building on the left is the former Baptist chapel on South Street, which has now been converted into flats. The field to the right is Hampden Meadow, which was given to Wendover as a recreation ground between the wars by the Barlow family who lived at Boswells. It was once used for football matches and sports days by the children of the Church of England School.

A multi-view postcard commemorating the 'Battle of the Hills', 21 June 1906. Long before the Mass Trespasses on Kinder Scout in the 1930s, the parishioners of Wendover took on the might of the Attorney General of England and Wales, Sir John Lawson Wharton, in order to protect their rights of way – and they won. Sir John owned a large house and grounds on Coombe Hill beneath the Monument and wished to prevent members of the public walking through his land to reach the Monument. To this end he erected stiles and fences to guide walkers away from his land, and put up signs telling them that they had no right of way along the old footpath. The people of Wendover fought this imposition and gave the Attorney General seven days in which to remove the offending structures. Sir John did not oblige, so the villagers walked one day *en masse* towards the monument and ripped down the stiles and fences as the police stood by helplessly. The victorious protesters then sang the National Anthem in loyal fashion. Afterwards Sir John agreed to dedicate the top of Coombe Hill to the people and put up a kissing gate to allow them access.

The Monument on Coombe Hill. It was erected to commemorate those who gave their lives in the Boer War in South Africa, 1899-1902.

In the late 1930s the Coombe Hill Monument was struck by lightning and almost completely destroyed. Buckinghamshire County Council agreed to undertake the restoration, which was completed in 1939. The Monument then had to spend the next six years under camouflage to prevent its use by enemy aircraft as a guide during the Second World War.

Looking up to Coombe Hill today from Butlers Cross, with the restored Monument clearly visible on the summit. The view from the Monument is extensive – on a good day one can look out over five counties: Bedfordshire, Buckinghamshire, Hertfordshire, Oxfordshire and Northamptonshire.

Sheep being driven up Bacombe Hill on the way to Ellesborough, in the days when centuries-old drove routes were still in use by farmers. At the time of writing, much is happening on Bacombe Hill. Heavy equipment has been moved in to help with conservation, and much of the undergrowth is being cleared and tidied up.

The road junction below Coombe Hill on the road from Chequers to Wendover.

Mavis, Susan and Danny Dabrowski outside their house at Calloway on Boddington Hill in 1953.

Boddington Hill from Wendover.

View from Oxon Hill, Wendover,
Showing York Buildings and Bacombe Hill.

The Tring Road and the outskirts of Wendover from Oxon Hill in the 1920s. This view is now completely different: the cornfields shown here have been replaced by the houses of the Honeydene estate.

Chequers, the country home of the Prime Minister, is just over the hill from Wendover towards Ellesborough. It was given to the country by Lord Lea of Fareham and has since played host to many a world leader. This view shows a gathering at the main entrance during the 1960s.

Chequers from the air, showing the many-gabled roofs and ornate, formal gardens.

The rear frontage of Chequers and the extensive lawns.

The interior of one of the sumptuously decorated rooms at Chequers.

Nine

And so to Halton

The Royal Artillery on training manoeuvres before the First World War.

Halton House, from the garden side. Note the ornate fountain in the gardens carved with mythical beasts and gods. This is Rothschild country: in addition to Halton and their main residence at Tring, they built mansions at Wing and Waddesdon.

The main entrance and frontage of Halton House, sometime between the wars. At this time the house was being used as the officers' mess, while the men were accommodated in huts (or even tents) in the grounds. Note the ornate architectural style, with columns, spires and a variety of window shapes.

Royal and other important visitors were frequently seen at Halton, both when it was occupied by the Rothschilds and later, when dignitaries came to review the troops. This shows a garden party in the grounds, with the house behind. When there were royal visitors, they were accompanied along the road from Wendover station by a military band.

Halton village by the canal bridge in Edwardian times. At this stage Halton House was still used by the Rothschilds and many of the villagers would have been employed by them as gardeners and household servants or would have worked for firms concerned with the upkeep of the house and gardens.

We're doing our Duty for KING and COUNTRY at WENDOVER

Birds Eye from Monument.

A patriotic postcard of Wendover country from the First World War. 'Tommies' from all over the country – and even further afield – came to Halton and Wendover to train and may have sent postcards like this to their loved ones.

CAMP LIFE AT HALTON PARK.

The ordinary soldiers were housed in tents like these while undergoing their training.

A group of officers surveying the camp from a convenient vantage point. Note their 'swagger sticks' which mark them out as being of high rank. The private soldiers' tents are situated a fair distance from the officers' mess in the house itself.

Field Marshal Lord Kitchener, Minister of War in Asquith's government in 1914, was responsible for the famous poster campaign calling men to join the Army – 'Your Country Needs You.'

After victory in 1918, the training camp at Halton became obsolete. The Rothschilds granted permission for the house and grounds to become an RAF training camp. Workshops such as these were erected in the grounds to repair aircraft and train aircraft apprentices. The camp was then designated No. 1 School of Technical Training.

The workshops today.

Inside the RAF workshops between the wars. This is 'advanced training' in carpentry skills. The structure being built by the group nearest to the camera appears to be a wing. In those days, virtually all carpentry jobs would have been done by hand, so precision training was vital in ensuring the reliability of the aircraft maintained at the camp.

Bullback Barracks from Boddington Hill. This is one of a number of barrack blocks built to house the burgeoning population of RAF Halton. No longer were servicemen expected to live in tents!

A general view of Halton Camp from Wendover Woods. In the distance is the Vale of Aylesbury.

The aerodrome and one of the hangars at Halton. This is situated on the Aylesbury side of the camp, beyond Halton village. Pilots flew on Avros and other small aircraft.

Commemoration of the sixth anniversary of the Armistice, 11 November 1924. For such occasions, as well as for inspections and passing out parades, it was customary to invite a dignitary – perhaps a member of the Royal Family or a senior RAF officer. Note that in this photograph the servicemen are all wearing 'fly-away' breeches and puttees on their lower legs. Thankfully these uncomfortable garments were abolished in favour of ordinary trousers by the time of the photograph opposite.

An inspection of apprentices (No. 2 Entry, No. 2 Section) at Halton, 7 March 1925. In more recent times, Her Majesty the Queen has been twice to Halton to present the Queen's Colour to the apprentices.

Passing out parades – at which newly qualified aircraft engineers commemorated their success – were important events at the No. 1 School of Technical Training. Afterwards there was always the obligatory group photograph. This is a group of cadets probably from the 1930s.

Isolation Hospital and Married Quarters, Halton.

This view of Halton Camp from 1934 shows the diversity of buildings contained within it. As well as hangars, workshops, runways and parade grounds there were all the buildings necessary to allow hundreds of servicemen to sleep and live there. Hence there are barracks, married quarters, provisions stores and a hospital. The hospital, Princess Mary's RAF Hospital, was demolished in the late 1990s.